MW01096340

D.R.O.P.S.

DAILY
REAL
OPTIMISTIC
POWER
STATEMENTS

Lord Milán L'Oiseau

ISBN: 978-1-4834-8739-7 (sc)
ISBN: 978-1-4834-8738-0 (e)

Lulu Publishing Services rev. date: 7/13/2018

Thank you to the known
and the unknown.

DAY 1

"If you can't see yourself as that thing, then don't even bother."

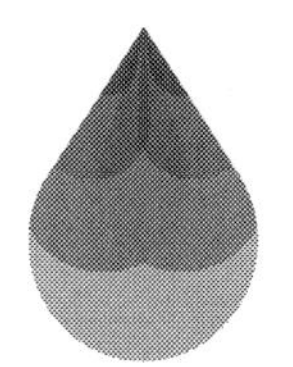

DAY 1

"Start your day expecting amazing things to happen to you because it's not about how many times amazing things happen, but that your eyes are open to see everything as amazing."

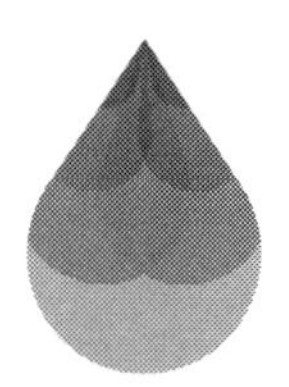

DAY 1

"Only after you refuse to be your own obstacle can you start the journey to become your greatest self."

DAY 1

"The best me, has nothing to do with you"

DAY 1

"Live in a constant state of
habitual betterment"

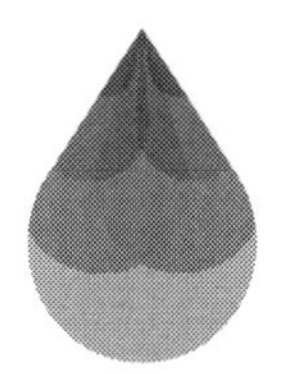

DAY 1

"Whatever you cannot imagine
you will NEVER see"

DAY 1

"What would happen if you
were YOUR best?"

DAY 1

"Someone needs the exact you, you are right now."

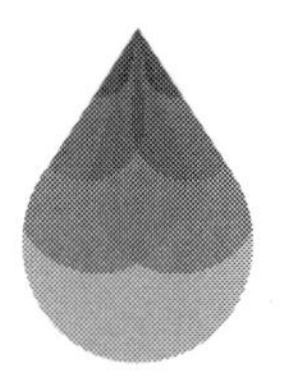

DAY 1

"You are what you choose to accept
and what you refuse to give up."

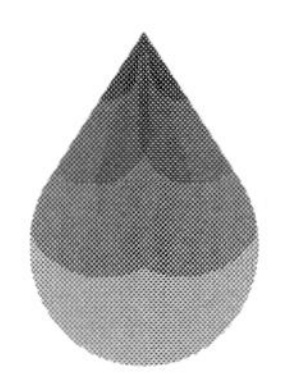

DAY 1

"Start your day expecting amazing things to happen to you because it's not about how many times amazing things happen, but that your eyes are open to see everything as amazing."

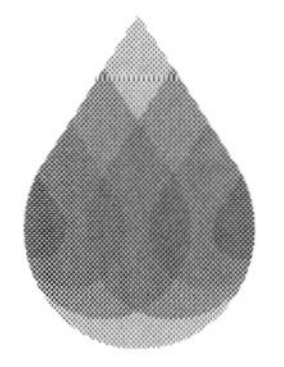
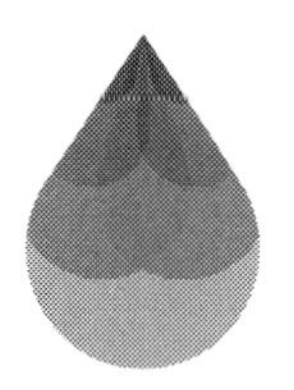

DAY 1

"Suffering caries within it the means to end suffering."

DAY 1

"The universe will test you just to see if you are ready for the next level."

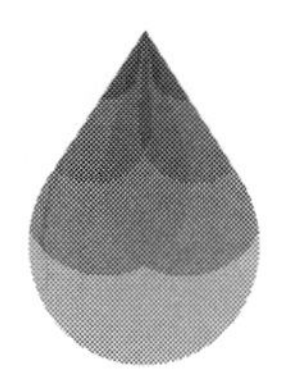

DAY 1

"When you put effort into yourself you always win."

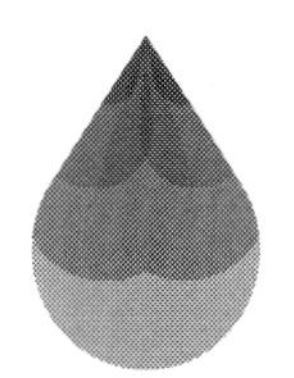

DAY 1

"Stop resisting your own greatness,
it's already a part of you."

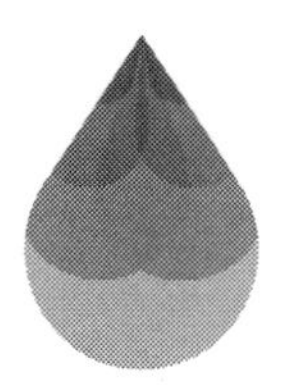

DAY 1

"Nothing that gets you closer
to your goal is a sacrifice."

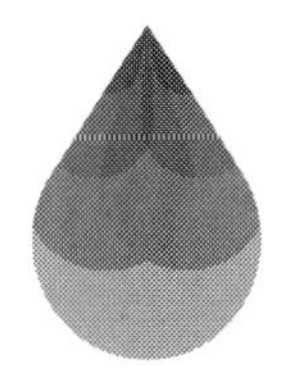

DAY 1

"You have the power to never let yourself down."

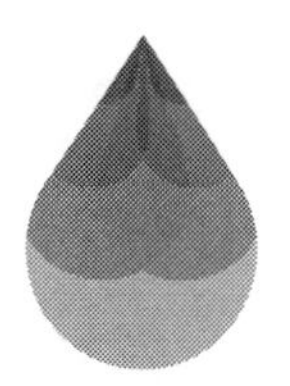

DAY 1

"Life is much less rewarding
as someone else."

DAY 1

"The opposite of love is fear. Don't be afraid to act on what's needed, even if it's only within yourself."

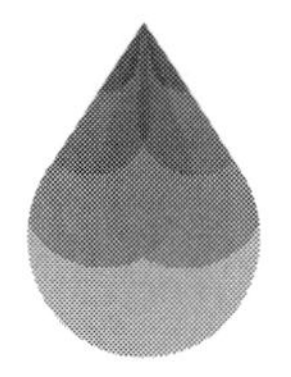

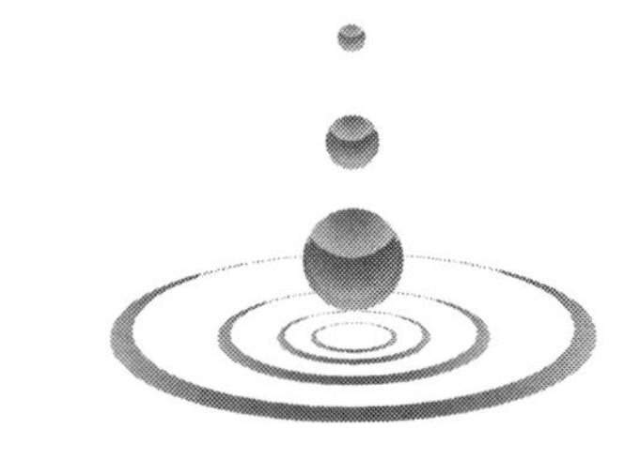

DAY 1

"Never start anything with a complaint."

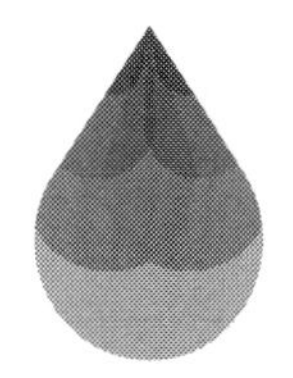

DAY 1

"Unless you follow up your thoughts with hard work, wishing won't help anything. Wishes are free. Success is not."

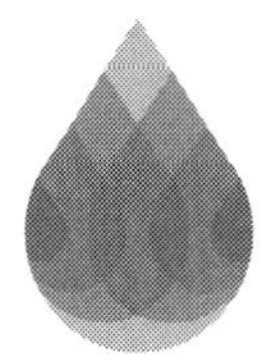
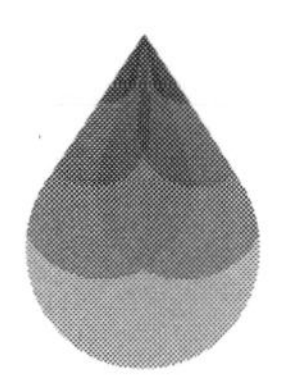

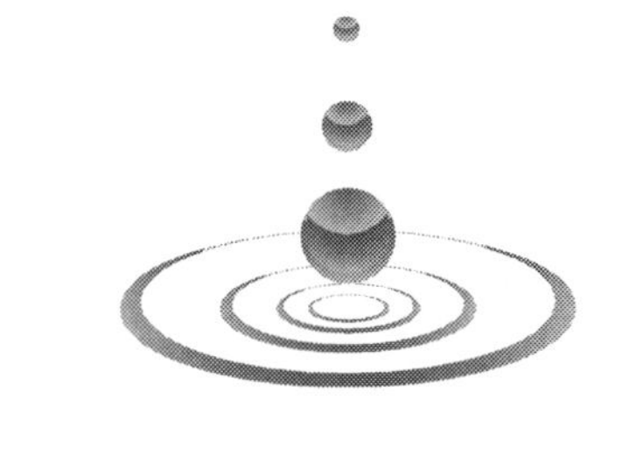

DAY 1

"Stop wishing."

DAY 1

"Your reality should be a
reflection of your dreams."

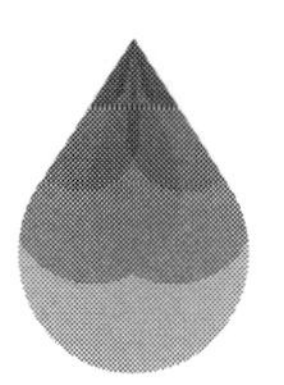

DAY 1

"Belief gives hard times meaning."

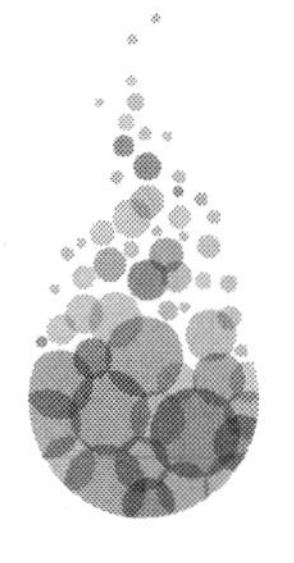

DAY 1

"Never add to the suffering."

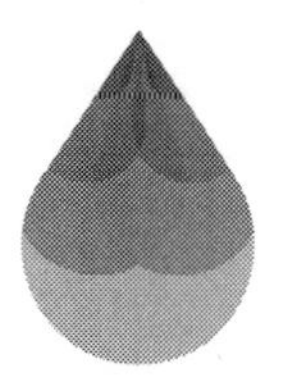

DAY 1

"Your skin tone and your talents
ARE mutually exclusive."

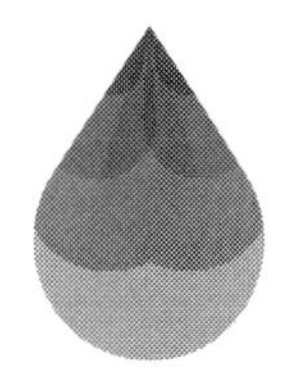

DAY 1

"Being consumed with the process
will blind you to the experience."

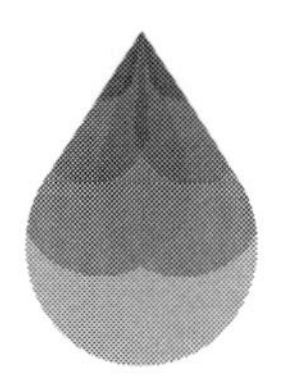

DAY 1

"When there is love in you and around you, all the hardship becomes meantime."

DAY 1

"Success is not comparable but rather uniquely positioned for the individual in order to create a positive ripple effect."

DAY 1

"Tired is never an excuse to quit."

DAY 1

"Be more concerned with the person you create rather than the person you find. That way you'll always find happiness."

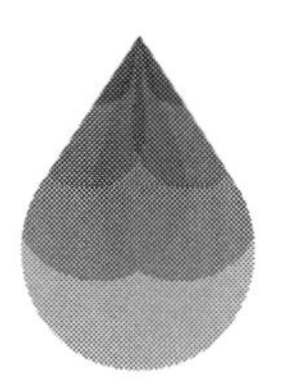

DAY 1

"Your tongue is your life's paintbrush."

DAY 1

"Happiness comes when you embrace your faults and live in your talents."

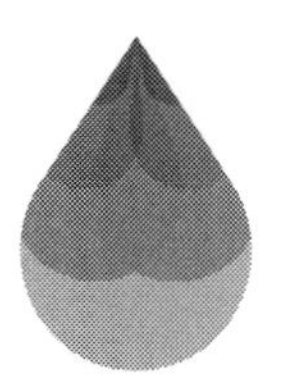

DAY 1

"Without scary things no one would ever have the chance to be brave."

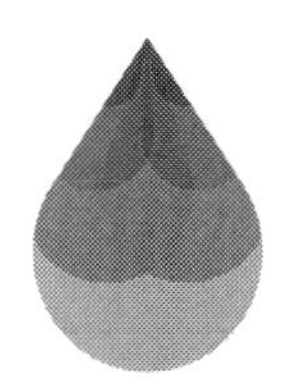

DAY 1

"There are people available to
you that can ensure your success.
It's up to you to access them."

DAY 1

"We all need someone around
that expects us to be great."

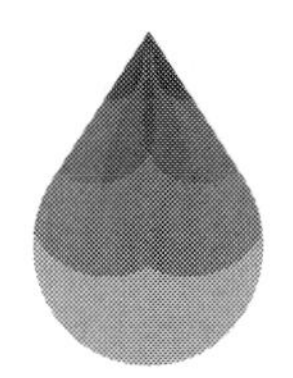

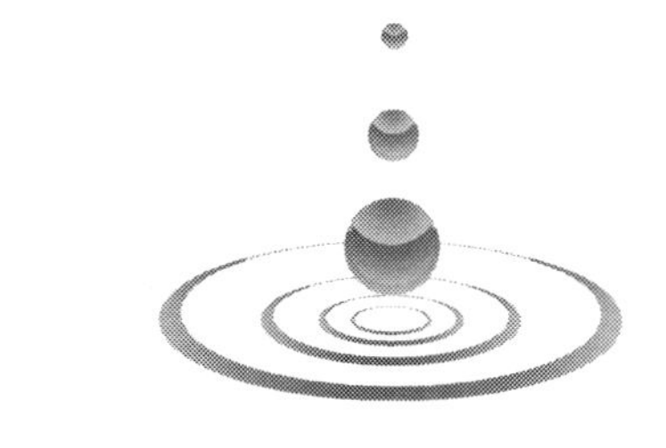

DAY 1

"Lessons bring blessings."

DAY 1

"Taking what seems like senseless pain
and giving it meaning is a powerful
tool to obtaining real happiness."

DAY 1

"If you don't really know yourself,
what can you really expect from you,
other than random decisions that
create something unrecognizable?"

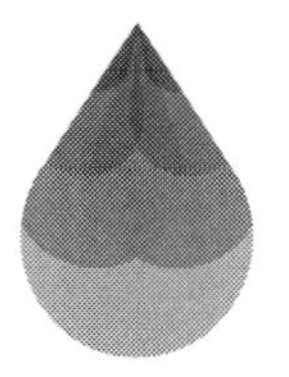

DAY 1

"Entertainment can profoundly affect your inner most thoughts and wishes. Therefore be mindful of what you choose to occupy yourself."

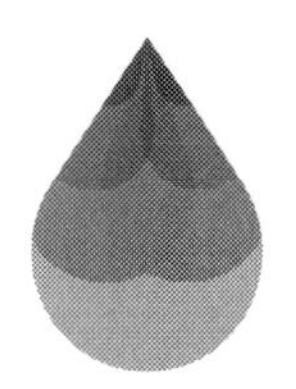

DAY 1

"If you have been inspired you have
the responsibility to inspire."

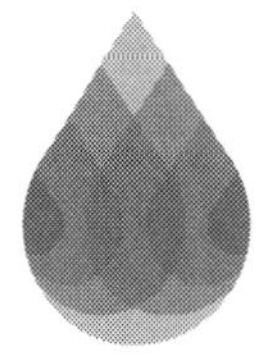
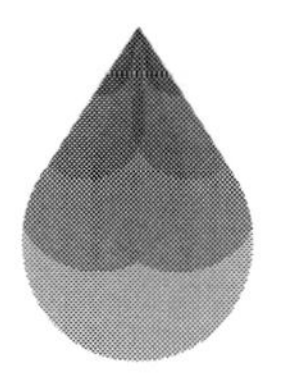

DAY 1

"When you avoid difficulty rather than embracing it, you prevent its true purpose which is to sharpen you for your future."

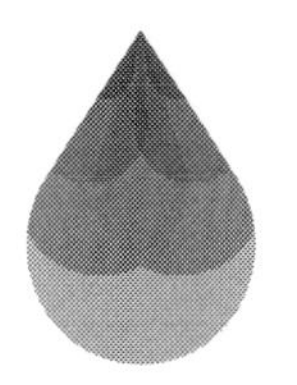

DAY 1

"When you close yourself off to the noise of the world you open yourself up to God."

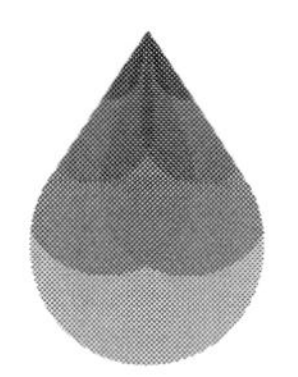

DAY 1

"Do things that matter to you."

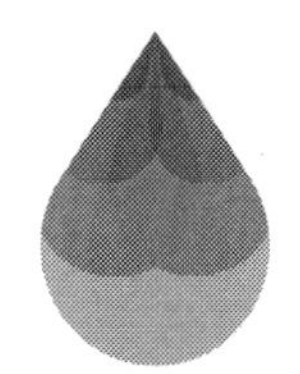

DAY 1

"Your habits shape your life. New habits will change the direction of your life."

DAY 1

"Success is not a place but rather a
conscience decision to better oneself
while acknowledging the bigger picture."

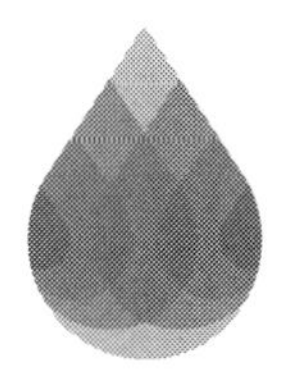
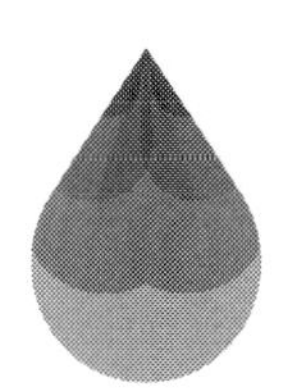

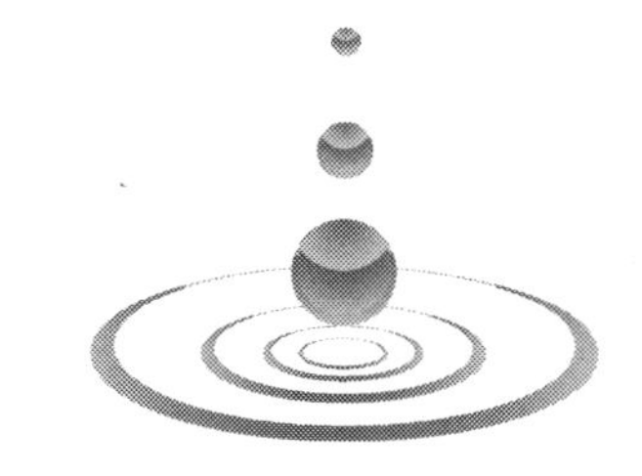

DAY 1

"Fear is really a lie trying to convince you that you are not as powerful as you are."

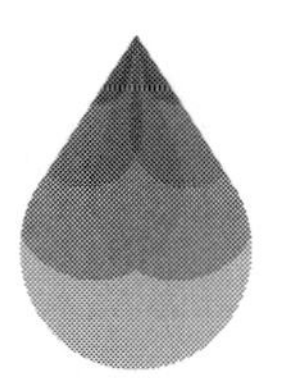

DAY 1

"Failures can serve as steps toward success as long as your eyes stay fixed on the ultimate goal."

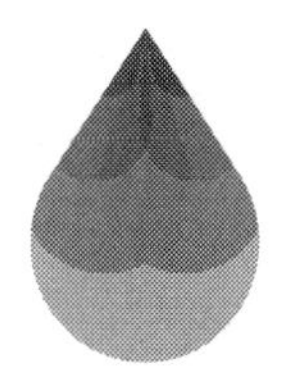

DAY 1

"Happiness is a reflection
of an honest you."

DAY 1

"Stressful times won't last forever, not even close to it. Remember that you control you, not your circumstances."

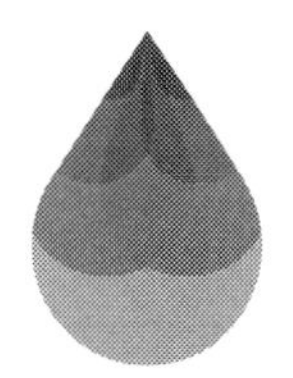

DAY 1

"Your life is a story meant to be rewritten over again endlessly as you pursue the promises of God."

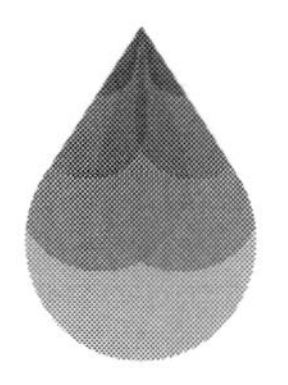

DAY 1

"That fear you feel is NOT real."

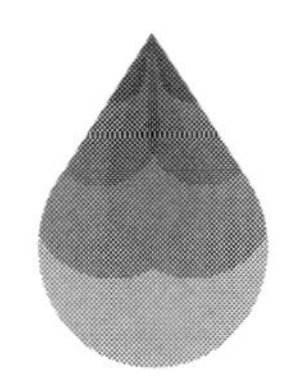

DAY 1

"When you are strong enough to remove your own darkness you become someone else's light."

DAY 1

"Embrace your can-do's, because when you do you will see how capable you really are and that can't is just an idea."

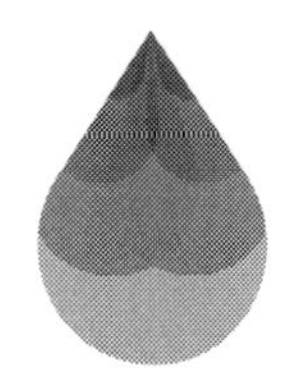

DAY 1

"The things that bother you are the things you're meant to do something about. Embrace them because your success means a better world."

DAY 1

"It's not our wounds but how we choose
to heal them that defines us."

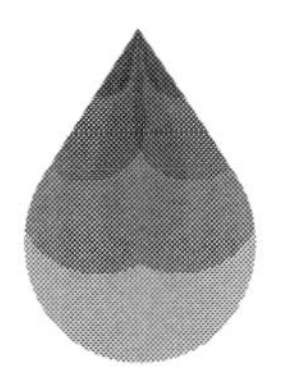

DAY 1

"This is how you know I love you, everything you want for yourself I want for you."

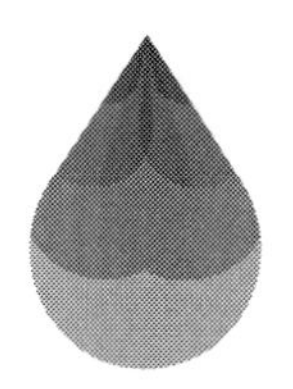

DAY 1

"The power that's in you to become and live your best life outweighs all the negativity that was, is, or will be."

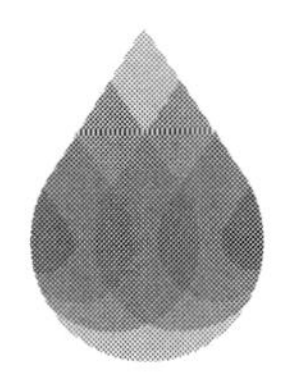

DAY 1

"The ability to get fed up is a powerful tool for change, betterment and success."

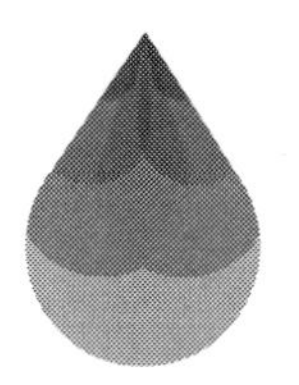

DAY 1

"Let your journey become a
message of hope for a stranger."

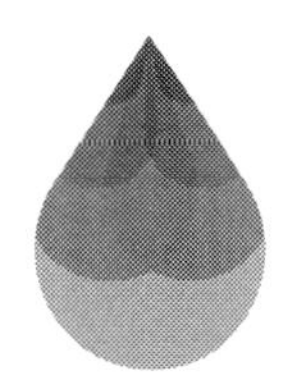

DAY 1

"Tomorrow is always a maybe.
Today is your only definite."

DAY 1

"You're old enough to
pursue your dreams."

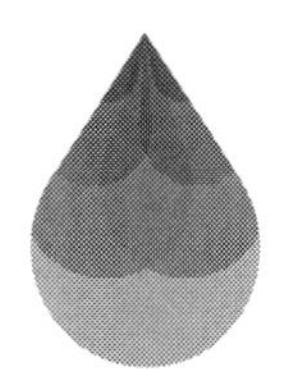

DAY 1

"Courage is necessary."

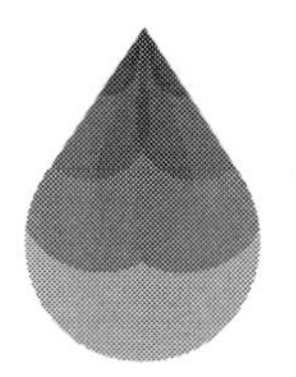

DAY 1

"Set your mind to greatness."

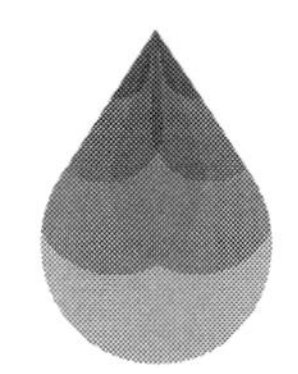

DAY 1

"Challenging times awake us and amplify our awareness of needing God's help."

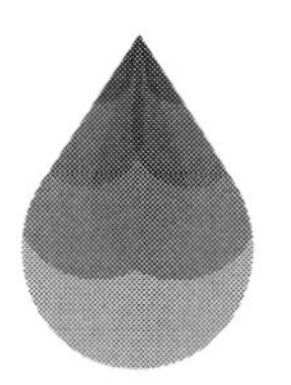

DAY 1

"Are you getting what you want out of yourself?"

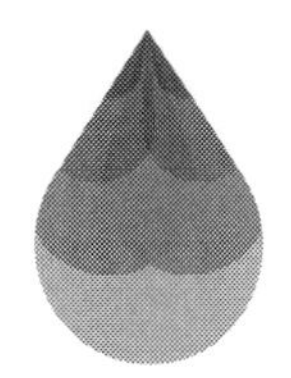

DAY 1

"Motivation is a choice before it's a habit, then finally a part of you."

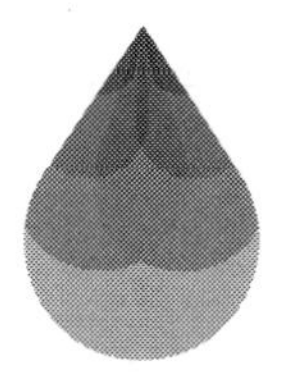

DAY 1

"The ability to achieve does not equal achievement."

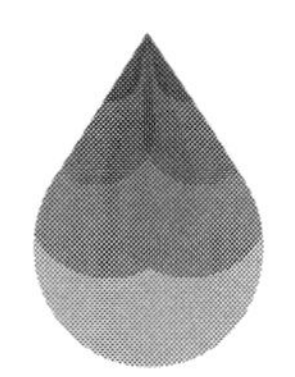

DAY 1

"Escaping your past without
examining your participation leads
to spiritual sepsis that needs purging
in order to embrace the new you."

DAY 1

"Be careful what you trade for a lie."

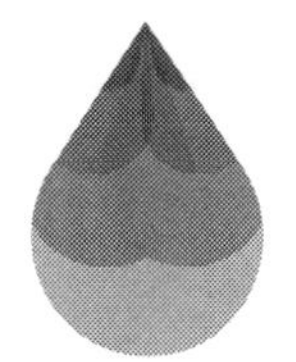

DAY 1

"Preparation is success in training."

DAY 1

"Regret is an inner voice calling,
not to look back and wallow in
negativity, but rather to tell you that
you still can find greatness."

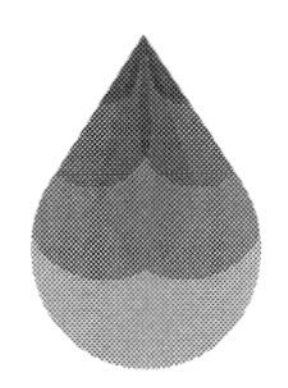

DAY 1

"Sometimes you have to get uncomfortable in order to know where change is needed in your life."

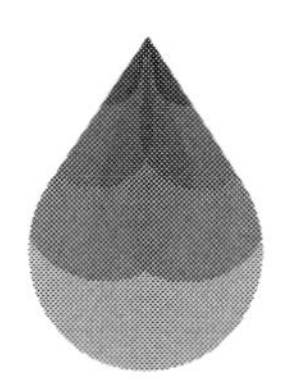

DAY 1

"Reality without 'I' is just a place.
Therefore you, make all the difference."

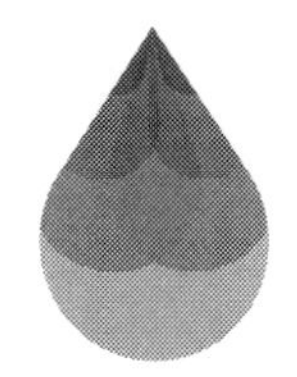

DAY 1

"If you believe something is okay as long as no one knows, you really believe something is wrong."

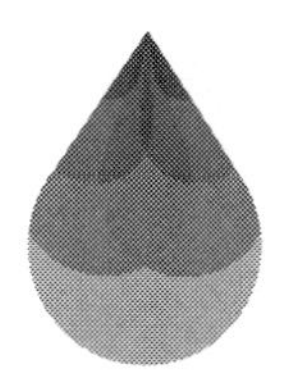

DAY 1

"Your words wield powerful consequences."

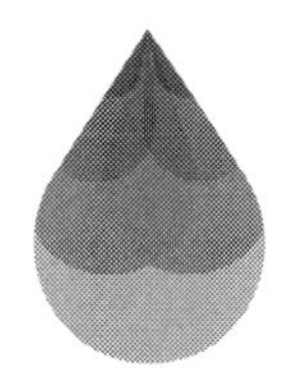

DAY 1

"You are stronger than
today's challenges."

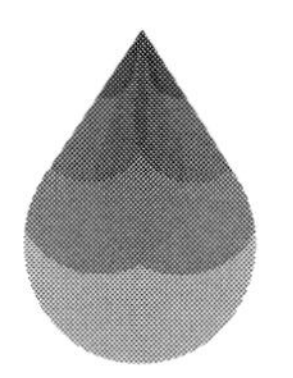

DAY 1

"Carpe diem doesn't mean
completing a to-do list but rather
recognizing the unique beauty
of this one of a kind 24hrs."

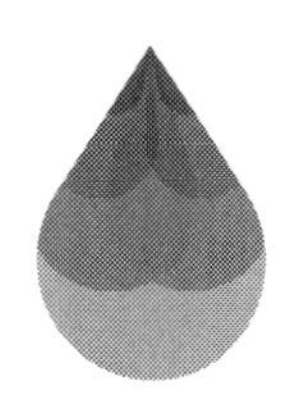

DAY 1

"If there were no more tomorrows
what would you have done today?"

DAY 1

"Starting over doesn't mean giving up. You are simply reattacking that mountain from a better vantage point."

DAY 1

"Make the change that makes you better."

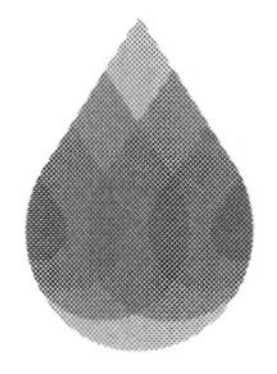
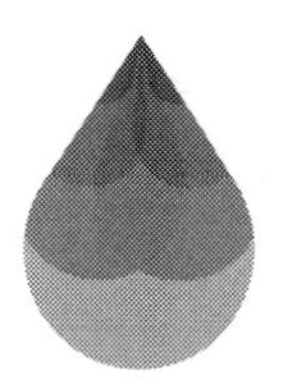

DAY 1

"Remember that your dreams came from you. So don't look to someone else to complete them."

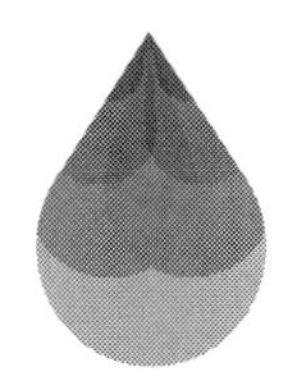

DAY 1

"Ask yourself to give you the things that you want out of life, not anyone else."

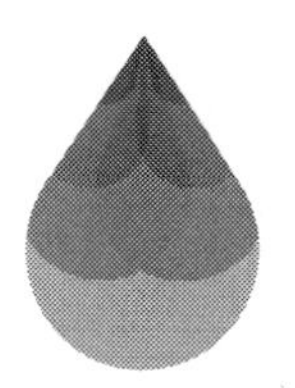

DAY 1

"Wishing requires 0% effort.
That's why it has 0% results."

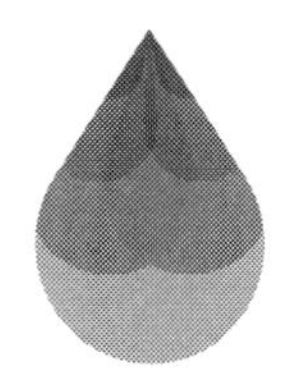

DAY 1

"Working towards where you want to be is the fastest way to get there."

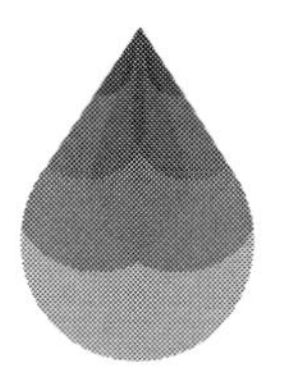

DAY 1

"Be your own competition and watch envy turn into self-fulfillment."

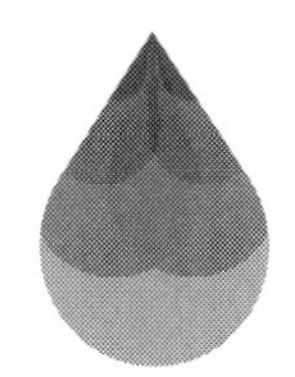

DAY 1

"The most important person to keep your promises to is yourself."

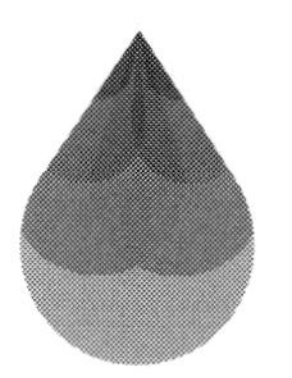

DAY 1

"Don't let fear of losing hold you back but rather push you to excel to the place where fear can't touch you."

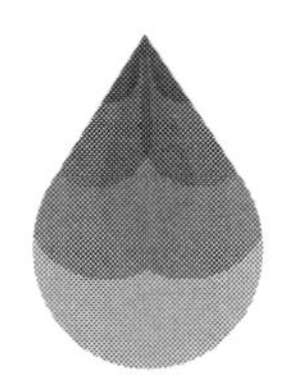

DAY 1

"Don't concern yourself with being wise but rather be willing to accept wisdom as it comes, no matter the source."

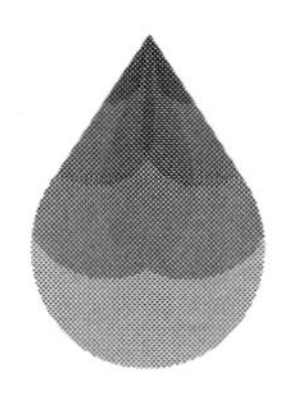

DAY 1

"Belief is contingent on one person YOU."

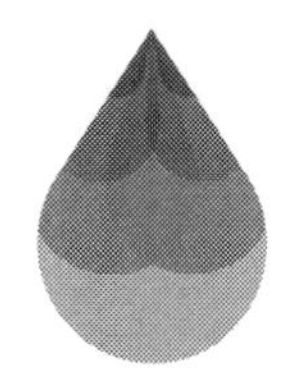

DAY 1

"You must learn, research, and trust in yourself. That way the opinions of others will never sway your truth."

DAY 1

"11:59pm went by, 12:00am means you can turn no into yes, fall into rise, fail into success. Today just started."

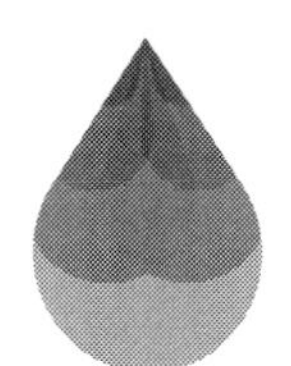

DAY 1

"Insight comes from those who
have experienced darkness
and made their way out."

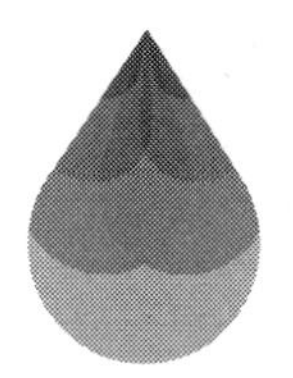

DAY 1

"Create a story that ends well."

DAY 1

"Discomfort usually means it's time
and possible to make your life better."

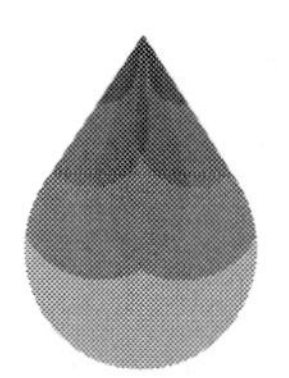

DAY 1

"When your pride lessens, your perspective grows."

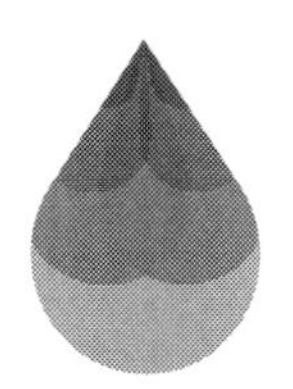

DAY 1

"If and IS are completely different. Choose the latter."

DAY 1

"Instead of saying what upsets or bothers you today, say 'they tried' to upset and bother you. Then watch how your spirit thrives."

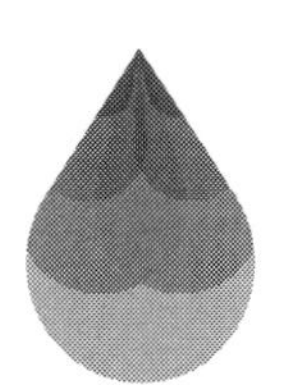

DAY 1

"You need faults and failures in order to want, desire, crave, love, fight for, then, take hold of YOUR success."

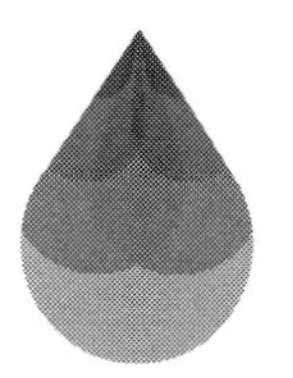

DAY 1

"A dream completed will always
lead to a dream completed."

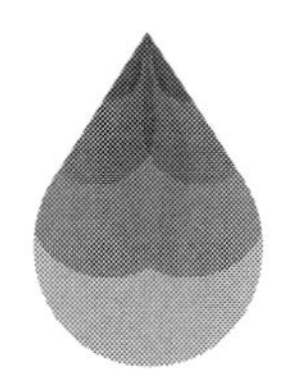

DAY 1

"A great leader is like a match, willing to give his all to light the way for another."

DAY 1

"Whose life are you living, yours
or the idea of someone else's?"

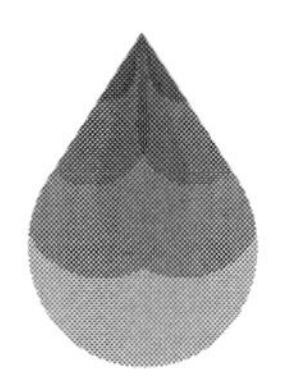

About the Author

The accident that rendered him a quadriplegic only motivated him to become a highly sought after Spanish professor and fashion designer with global influence. The quotes in this book have served him and now serve others on their journey.

Made in the USA
Lexington, KY
27 March 2019